Daniel Folkmar

The Duration of School Attendance in Chicago and Milwaukee

Daniel Folkmar

The Duration of School Attendance in Chicago and Milwaukee

ISBN/EAN: 9783337812409

Printed in Europe, USA, Canada, Australia, Japan

Cover: Foto ©Paul-Georg Meister /pixelio.de

More available books at **www.hansebooks.com**

THE DURATION OF SCHOOL ATTENDANCE IN CHICAGO AND MILWAUKEE.

BY

DANIEL FOLKMAR,

*Late Lecturer in Social Science, University of Chicago,
Fellow of Royal Statistical Society, etc.*

READ BEFORE THE WISCONSIN ACADEMY OF SCIENCES,
DECEMBER 28, 1897.

TABLE OF CONTENTS.

TABLES.

THE DURATION OF SCHOOL ATTENDANCE IN CHICAGO AND MILWAUKEE.

(WITH DIAGRAM—PLATE I.)

DANIEL FOLKMAR.

IMPORTANCE OF THE QUESTION.

Is not the question of all questions in education how to retain our pupils through more years of schooling? If it can be shown that pupils reach, on the average, only the third or fourth grade before dropping out, have we not missed the most essential point by putting the great emphasis now-a-days upon methods? Is not the real question, not *how* shall we teach, but how *much* shall we teach? If the average pupil has only time allowed him to acquire the elements of the three "R's," have we not erred in crowding them aside by "enriching the curriculum" with nature study and other new applicants for favor? Has not Dr. Harris rightly interpreted the needs of civilization in his restoration of reading, writing, and arithmetic to the leading place in the course of study?[1]

These fundamental questions depend so largely upon the actual amount of schooling that we can count upon in the case of the average child, that much effort would be justified in attempting to determine the latter. There is probably nowhere in educational literature a scientific demonstration of the number that drop permanently out of school at the close of each grade.

The aim of this paper is indicated above. It is to ascertain at what grade the pupils in the public schools drop out — what per cent. go no further than the first grade, what per cent. stop with the second grade, what per cent. with the primary school,

---

[1] "Report of the Committee of Fifteen" in the *Proceedings* of the National Educational Association, 1895, pp. 290-6.

17

what per cent. with the grammar school, and what per cent. reach
the high school.

By a comparison of the facts thus ascertained with the statistics of other cities and of the United States as a whole, a
somewhat definite idea can be formed as to the total amount
of schooling received by each citizen —a fact of high importance to the educator and to the sociologist.

The only exact method, but at present an impossible one,
would be to take a complete census of the population above the
school age, ascertaining in each individual case the grade with
which schooling ceased. Another method, quite as impossible,
would be to tabulate the school records previous to 1885, let us
say, tracing the history of each individual whose name appears
upon them.   As a matter of fact, the Great Fire of Chicago and
the previous existence of a ten-grade system in each city, make
this method out of the question.

Reserving further suggestions upon methods, ideal or other-
wise, until a later stage of the discussion, I will pass at once
to an explanation of the methods which were actually employed
in this investigation.

It is evident that the only method that will cover so great a
multitude of cases is the statistical. Since the method of mere
enumeration could not be employed, resource was had to deductions from such statistics as were available. Two main lines or
methods of demonstration were employed in the study of each
city, the one serving as a check upon the other. They may be
designated as: (1) the Deductive, or Enrollment, method; (2) the
Inductive, or Class, method.

In the first, the enrollments by grades for one year or the
totals for a group of years, are made the basis of deduction or
inference as to the per cents that must have dropped out from
the lower grades; in the second, the enrollment of a single class
entering the first grade is followed from grade to grade through
the reports of successive years, the number that drop out at
each grade is noted, and from a comparison of the corresponding facts in the history of other classes, a generalization is

reached inductively as to the normal number that drop out at each grade.

There are, therefore, four groups of tables in the study of the two cities, with a fifth group which compares the conclusions thus reached with the facts collected from other cities and writers. Admitting errors in each method employed, secondary tables and considerations have been introduced: on the one hand to eliminate errors so far as possible; on the other hand to determine the limits of probable error, so that if per cents could not be determined with absolute accuracy, statements could at least be made as to the maximum and minimum limits within which the truth lay.

Neither through my present acquaintance with statistical methods nor through the co-operation of a university instructor in statistics, have I been enabled to find methods ready-made which were applicable to this problem. The only resource was one not uncommon in scientific work, a slow process of trial and experimentation, during which more time was spent upon the rejected methods than upon those finally adopted.[1]

SOURCES OF INFORMATION.

To assist any who may wish to use the same material, and also to explain the data upon which my inferences are based, a brief statement may be made at this point as to the sources of information. A large portion of the data concerning the Chicago schools was taken from the Annual Reports of the Board of Education, beginning with the year after the Great Fire, 1871-72, which destroyed all the previous records. Since the year 1888-89, unfortunately, the school enrollment by grades has not been printed, — which fact necessitated (in 1894 at the

---

[1] Thanks are due to Dr. Hourwich of the University of Chicago for valued assistance; also to Mrs. Stevens, statistician of the Chicago Board of Education, in allowing me to copy the annual returns in advance of her own elaboration of them for the Annual Report, and especially in loaning me the bulky files of the years 1889-93, which are the only data now in existence from which may be obtained the grade enrollments for these four important years. Most important of all was the co-operation of Mrs. Folkmar on the Milwaukee portion of the work, since she not only elaborated the most of the material but added important theoretical suggestions.

time the Chicago portion of this paper was written) the weari-
some copying for many days of the manuscript reports of over
two hundred principals for the years 1889–94 and the adding
of endless columns.   The figures published herewith are,
therefore, the only ones to be found in print.[1]   The Chicago
data have not been brought down to the present year, since
this would necessitate not only special trips to Chicago but the
expenditure of a large amount of time in copying the manuscript files without materially changing the results already secured.   Neither had the enrollment previous to 1879–80 been
published by grades, although the same regularity noticeable
in it may be demonstrated as far back as 1875 from the data of
Table II, giving the average daily membership (Chicago),
1875–76 to 1880–81.[2]

Preceding 1875 the necessary comparisons cannot be made.
Since a ten-grade system was in vogue until that year, the per
cents before and after 1875 are incommensurable.   The fifteen
years, however, from 1880 to 1894 give a sufficient basis for
the deductions sought.

The Annual Reports of the School Board of Milwaukee are
still more unsatisfactory to the statistician than those of the
Chicago Board, since there never has been published a total
enrollment by grades since the twelve-grade system was introduced.   All that can be done, therefore, under the deductive or
enrollment method, is to tabulate the average enrollment since
the year just named, as is shown in the discussion of the table
(p. 263, *infra*).   However, the average enrollment is quite
satisfactory for comparison with the Chicago table of total enrollment.

---

[1] Table I.   *Enrollment of Public Schools (Chicago). Fifteen Years*,
p. 282 *infra*.   The data for this table, for the years 1880–89, are compiled
from tables in the appendixes of the annual reports; e. g. *Report* for 1889,
pp. 142 and 152.

[2] Page 283 *infra*.   The data for this table are compiled from tables in
the appendixes of the annual reports; e. g., *Report* for 1889, p. 146.

DEDUCTIVE METHOD.

Passing now to the deductive or enrollment method, the first form in which it was suggested in the investigation, seems rather too simple to be safe. Yet it must be retained, if only because of the ease with which it may be applied to the statistics of other cities, in making the broader generalizations which this paper suggests. It will be found, also, to be a much closer approximation to the truth than would at first thought appear. The method consists in a simple inference based upon the relatively small numbers constantly enrolled in the higher grades. A knowledge of this well-known fact leads every one to the conclusion, that a very large majority of the pupils fail to reach the high school, and that entirely too large a number drop out before reaching the grammar grades. That there is a fundamental and remarkably unyielding law corresponding to this opinion, is seen by massing the enrollment figures for the Chicago Schools as far back as they are available.[1]

Deductive Method Applied to Chicago. — It needs but a glance of the eye over the the table to discover that we have here an instance of the wonderful uniformity of the laws governing social phenomena. Notwithstanding the great fluctuations of population through immigration and exodus, the annexation of large districts, the transfer of pupils to and from parochial and private schools (which are one-half as large in number as the public schools of the city) and other social and economic disturbances, we find that the enrollment of no grade, with the exception of the first, has changed more than one per cent. from year to year. With substantially the same forces in operation during the succeeding fifteen years, we may feel sure that the same uniformity of attendance will be found as in the past fifteen. The slight tendency to increase or decrease in certain grades will continue. The inference suggested by merely a superficial glance at the figures (Table III) might be stated as follows: If, out of every 1,000 pupils, there never have been more than four pupils that reached the twelfth grade, the remaining 996 dropped out before reaching that grade. By the same reasoning

---

[1] Table III. *Per Cent. of Enrollment in each Grade* (Chicago), p. 284.

99 per cent. would be shown to have dropped out on an average before reaching the eleventh grade; 97 per cent. before reaching the high school; 77 per cent. before passing beyond the primary grades; and 32 per cent. before reaching the second grade. The next table would then show the per cents that dropped out at each grade during fifteen years.[1]

The same facts are more vividly shown to the eye by the following graphic representation (Diagram A.) The per cent. that never went beyond the limit of the first grade, the second grade, the third grade, and so on, are cut off by the heavy boundary lines.

Incidental Observations. — Some interesting facts may be noticed in passing, though they touch only indirectly upon the inductive method. In the first place, it will be seen from Table III that there has been for ten years past a slight but regular tendency toward decrease in the primary grades and a corresponding increase in the grammar and high school grades. The largest decrease has been in the first grade — from thirty-five to thirty per cent. The twelfth grade of the high school has made a corresponding increase from one-tenth to four-tenths of one per cent. This indicates that a slowly increasing number stay in school long enough to reach the grammar and high school grades; a fact which would be expected to accompany the increase of wealth and intelligence among the parents and the increasing educational demands of society upon the young. These laws of attendance evident during ten years, would no doubt hold good back to 1880. The apparent increase in the primary grades and decrease in the grammer grades in the five years following 1880, is explained by the superintendent of schools as being caused by the new method of promotion which went into effect at that time. Some time after dropping the examination system, it was found that principals were not making recommendations for promotion with sufficient freedom. Upon having the matter brought to their attention it was remedied, and the rate of promotion regained its old regularity. Yet from the curious fact, that in the culminating year of

---

[1] Table IV. *Per Cent. of Pupils that do not go beyond the Grade Named* (Chicago), p. 285.

Plate I.

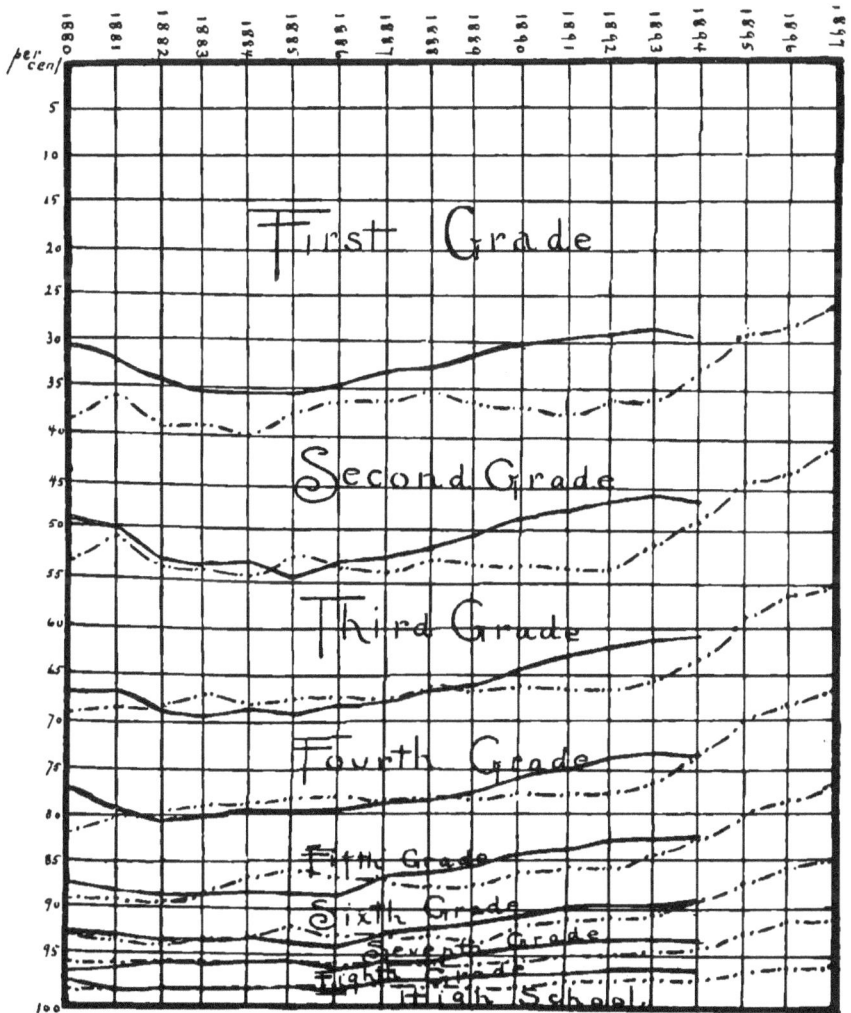

DIAGRAM A.—Showing what Per Cent. of the Population leaves School at each Grade.

Chicago, — —————— .

Milwaukee, —— · · —— · ·

the first grade, 1884, and the second grade, 1887, the same
phenomena were observable in Milwaukee (Table V), it would
appear that the cause was a wide-reaching social condition.
Since a larger per cent. in these grades indicates a smaller per
cent. in the grammar grades, what bearing does this fact have
on the theory that in "good times" advanced pupils do not
attend school so largely as in "bad times"?

At first thought it would seem that there are disturbing
factors which would render the apparent regularity of the figures impossible. Such are the death rate and fluctuations in
the population from annexation, immigration, and exodus. The
death rate, however, during school age, as we shall presently
see (p. 270), is so small as not to affect the results appreci-
ably; while, explain it as we may, the same wonderful regularity is found throughout the table despite the great increase in
immigration in recent years and such sudden changes as the
annexation of a large population in suburban districts in 1889
and 1890. The most reasonable hypothesis is, that additions
to the population brought with them the same normal per cents
of children to enter the various grades. It seems probable from
data adduced in subsequent pages (pp. 273-4) that not only other
parts of the United States but many countries of Europe, carry
education to about the same grades; so that pupils coming from
them to Chicago are simply transferred in grade. This is no
doubt almost absolutely true of the annexed districts.

Deductive Method Applied to Milwaukee. — The similarity of the
Milwaukee statistics may be seen by applying the same deductive method to them. As has already been said, the figures of
the actual enrollment in Milwaukee are not obtainable, but the
statistics of the "average enrollment" are in nearly enough the
same proportion to answer for the comparison.[1]

Since the per cents in the Milwaukee reports include the
kindergarten and exclude the high school, revised tables are
given, with reductions so made as to be comparable with the

[1] Table V. *Per Cent. of Enrollment in Each Grade* (Milwaukee), p. 286.
This table is compiled from the per cents given in the Statistical Tables
of the annual reports of the School Board — e. g., Report for 1895-96, p. 64.

Chicago tables.[1] Comparing the second of these tables with the corresponding Chicago table (IV, p. 285), it will be seen that the averages do not vary one and one-half per cent. in the two tables except in the first grade, which is three per cent. larger in the Milwaukee table. This slight excess is clearly due to the fact that we are dealing with true enrollment figures in the Chicago table but with "average" enrollments in the Milwaukee table.

Errors in Deductive Method.— But, however accurate and simple this method may be in reaching the per cent. that normally drops out at each grade, it must be justified by comparison with other methods. There are errors in it not easily eliminated; some of which would make the per cents too large, while other errors would make the per cents too small. Now, if we apply our corrections, for example, to the second grade (Table III or VI, *Per Cent. in each Grade*), it is evident that any error which makes it too small will make the per cents in the grammar grades too large, and *vice versa;* also that if the second grade per cent. is too small in this table, it is too small in the table derived from it, the first grade remaining unchanged. (Table IV or VII, *Per Cents that Drop Out.*)

One of the two largest errors makes the final second grade per cent. (the 50 per cent. that dropped out) too small. It arises from the fact that the base is too large. If the base were smaller the second grade per cents in both tables, as is shown above, would be larger. But the base should be smaller; for the grand total of the fifteen years' enrollment, one and one-half millions (compare Tables I and IX), is evidently not pupils, but pupil-grades, or enrollments; that is, the number of enrollments that would appear on the books in all the grades. Since most pupils have been enrolled in more than one grade, this number is three or four times the number of pupils.[2] The number of pupils

[1] Table VI. Same as Table V, *With Corrections for Kindergarten and High School,* p. 287. Table VII. *Per Cent. of Pupils that do not go beyond the Grades Named* (Milwaukee), p. 288. See, also, "Diagram A," facing p. 262.

[2] See discussion of the average number of grades each pupil has attended, p. 272.

would more nearly correspond to the total of the first grade, one-half million, on the supposition that all pupils were first enrolled in the first grade.

The other chief error, taken by itself, would make our final second grade per cent. too large — namely, the fact that our percentage[1] (282, 992), is too large. It is too large by approximately one-third, since about thirty-three per cent. of any second grade enrollment appear to be pupils who remain in the second grade two years (p. 267, *infra*).

The death rate and the fluctuations of population do not materially vitiate this method, as will be seen later (p. 270). The former is never an appreciable quantity, and the latter is inoperative because we are here dealing not with classes as they actually advance through the grades, but with the proportionate enrollments in the various grades at all times — and we might say in all places; for national and even European statistics correspond in a general way to those of Chicago and Milwaukee.[2] In the latter case, no matter how many families would remove to or from Chicago, it would not change the proportions that enroll in the various grades.

The most important correction, therefore, to be made under this method, is to eliminate the second enrollment that each pupil made in any grade. We could then be sure that we had reached the minimum limit in our second grade average; and could also compute the average number of grades that each pupil had attended. This brings us to one of the main topics of the paper.

IMPORTANCE OF DETERMINING LIMITS OF ERROR.

Let us stop to remind ourselves of the main aims of the paper. The first aim is to determine what per cent. of pupils drop out at each grade. This we seem already to have approximately secured, to judge by the methods discussed later, for they only corroborate the results of the deductive method. It seems that the errors which tended to make the per cents first

---

[1] This word is used throughout the paper in the strict sense to designate concrete numbers, not the corresponding per cents.

[2] See *Enrollment of Various Countries*, p. 273.

too large and next too small have neutralized each other. But, since this is after all only an approximation and not a perfect demonstration, the second great aim must be to determine the outside limits between which the truth must lie. The maximum limit will be reached under the inductive method. The minimum limit may be got at once by reducing percentages.

Minimum Limit of Error.— As was shown on page 264, if we reduce the percentages (the totals for the second and other grades in Table IX) without reducing the base (the one and one-half million grand total), or at least without reducing it in so great a ratio as the percentages, we shall reduce the rate per cents. But we know that the base is at least three times too large. (See p. 264). The question is how much to deduct from the apparent enrollments, especially in the first four grades, to make the numbers stand in the same relation to each other as do the true enrollments. That all the other grades are within from one to ten per cent. of the actual enrollment will probably be granted after the following discussion.

Correction for Double Enrollment. — The apparent or printed enrollment in each of these grades is too large, because many pupils are not only enrolled in them on entering the grade but also on coming back to it the next year — those pupils, namely, who failed of promotion. The determination of the number enrolled twice in each grade, is the most incomplete part of the present paper. It would seem to be impossible to get accurate results from the material at hand in Chicago and Milwaukee. The question is, therefore, turned over to the future investigator in this subject with the following imperfect data and inferences.

Since we are seeking only a limit of error, perhaps so large a reduction of the grades may be made that anything greater would be clearly unreasonable. The next table of promotions[1] is of prime importance. It can not be inferred, however, that all who fail of promotion were enrolled in the same grade for the following year. How many of these dropped out of

---

[1] Table VIII. *Number of Pupils Promoted* (Chicago), p. 289. This table is compiled from the Superintendent's Reports in the Annual Reports of the Board (e. g., report for 1897, p. 30.)

school altogether is the largest element of uncertainty. In the calculation, of course, the total number who dropped out at any grade is made up both from those who were promoted and those who failed of promotion. No exact determination of the number in either case can be made, but the following additional considerations may render our inferences more accurate.

We must begin with the enrollment of the grades as corrected for increase in population (Table XIV, and p. 268). If we subtract, for example, from the third grade enrolled in 1887 the number promoted from the second grade in 1886, we have left approximately the number that were enrolled a second time in 1887 in the third grade. This is about twenty-five per cent. of of the enrollment of 1886, and is about the average for the third grade, as will be found by trying different years. In the same way it will be found that a deduction of about 10 per cent. should be made from the fourth grade, 33 per cent. from the second grade, and 45 per cent. from the first grade to allow for double enroll-ments. Adding together our revised enrollments, we get a grand total of 1,270,000 (See Table IX. *True Enrollment*, p. 290). Since now we have made reductions of 10, 25, 33, and 45 per cent. in our percentages and a reduction of only 38 per cent. in our base, which was already three times too large (See p. 266), it must be admitted that the resulting per cents are the smallest possible.

Let us recapitulate the argument as regards the second grade. (1) We have as a base, 1,500,000, the total enrollment of all grades; as percentage, 282,000, the enrollment of the second grade; which is 18 per cent. of the total enrollment. (2) We have reduced the base to 1,270,000, while the true base, the number that entered the first grade, is nearer 500,000 (p. 264); we have reduced the percentage to 212,000 or 33 per cent., which is about the true percentage; giving 16 as our per cent. instead of 18. (3) But since we have reduced the percentage as much as possible and left the base far too large, the resulting per cent. must be too small; that is, the "16 per cent." of all that entered the first grade said to drop out in the second, is the smallest imaginable per cent., which was to be proven. The same is true of each of the other grades.

Conclusions as to Minimum Limit.—There can be no doubt, therefore, that at least the following per cents dropped out at the grades named:[1]

27   per cent. by the end of the first grade.

43   per cent. by the end of the second grade.

58   per cent. by the end of the third grade.

71   per cent. by the end of the fourth grade.

82   per cent. by the end of the fifth grade.

89   per cent. by the end of the sixth grade.

93   per cent. by the end of the seventh grade.

96   per cent. by the end of the eighth grade.

93   per cent. by the end of the ninth grade.

99   per cent. by the end of the tenth grade.

99.6 per cent. by the end of the eleventh grade.

100   per cent. by the end of the twelfth grade.

This is our minimum limit.

INDUCTIVE METHOD.

Let us now take up the second general method of the paper, the inductive or class method. The difficulty in following a particular class from grade to grade in these statistics is due to the increase of population through immigration. Many children on coming from other cities to Chicago, enter the higher grades, thus increasing the apparent number of the real class that entered in the first grade. The first thing necessary, therefore, is to make population-corrections in the class enrollment.

Corrections for Increase of Population.—The next three tables[2] will make clear the method used in ascertaining the corrections to be applied to the printed enrollment (Table XIII). Table X gives the official biennial census. The figures for the alternate years can easily be estimated by inspection, for the increase is found to follow a regular law. It is, for several years after 1880,

---

[1] Table IX, *True or Entrance Enrollment* (Chicago), p. 290; also Table XXIII, *Final Conclusions as to Per Cents that Drop Out*, page 304.

[2] Table X, *Method of Obtaining Population Corrections*, p. 291; Table XI., *Population Corrections*, p. 292; Table XII, *Estimated Per Cents of Increase of Population*, p. 293.

7 per cent. of the population of 1880, then running up to 13 per cent. in 1892. The only exceptions are two great increases of about 60 per cent. and 20 per cent. respectively, caused by the annexation of large out-lying districts to the city in 1890 and in 1891.

In a similar way the population-corrections for the other columns are found (Table XI, p. 292). The per cents in bold faced type are exact, being derived immediately from the official census. The rest of the table is estimated. Quite evident laws are discovered by mere inspection of Table XII (p. 293), where these factors are analyzed — regularities of increase and decrease vertically, horizontally, and diagonally across the table being evident. We are thus enabled to fill in the alternate columns (Table XI) with tolerable assurance.

Having this law of the increase of population, it will easily be seen that corresponding deductions should be made from the enrollments of classes through the successive grades, since the incoming population brings pupils that enter the different grades in about the same proportion as that in which the Chicago pupils are distributed among them. Table XIII (p. 294) gives the enrollment of each class as it passes through the successive grades. Table XIV (p. 295) gives the true enrollment as corrected for increase of population. Subtracting the enrollment of the second grade from that of the first, gives us the number that dropped out of school at the first grade. Going through the entire table in this same way, we get Table XV. *Number That Dropped out by End of Each Grade* (p. 296). From these numbers taken as percentages with the corresponding first grade enrollment taken as a base, we get Table XVI. *Per Cent. of First Grade Enrollment Dropped out by End of Each Grade* (p. 297).

Although this method seems the most direct and exact, it will be seen that the per cents are unexpectedly large. It will also be seen that we have very uniform laws evident throughout these years as to the per cent. that drops out at each grade. The average for each period of four years makes this clear.[1]

---

[1] Table XVII. *Average Per Cent. of First Grade Enrollment Dropped out by End of Each Grade* (Chicago), p. 298.

Corrections for Death.—Another factor should be given consideration in this inductive method, namely, the per cents that drop out through death. What correction, if any, should be made in the table for this cause? A table of the death rate per thousand will make it evident that the correction would not be an appreciable quantity. We may take, for instance, the English Life Table No. III, which is a standard authority in life insurance [1] and we shall find that during the school age, 7 to 18 years, less than one per cent. drop out in any year on account of death, (more exactly, from .9 per cent. of the first grade enrollment in the first year to .006 per cent. of it in the twelfth grade) and putting that small correction beside the large per cents, 43, 54, 66, and the rest in Table XVI, it is evident that the correction is of no practical importance.

Inductive Method in Milwaukee.—The Milwaukee statistics cannot be used directly and with entire satisfaction in this inductive method, for the actual enrollment of the grades has never been printed. The "average enrollment" which we have in the reports is a different matter. Still, if it is necessary, the actual enrollment might be estimated on the basis of the average enrollment. This will hardly be necessary after having the Chicago results, for we may see at once from the tables of average enrollments that the enrollments stand in almost exactly the same ratio throughout the tables as do the Chicago enrollments; and we might get the per cents that dropped out in each grade directly from them — but with the understanding that the per cents are much too large. We are unable to reduce the higher grades for increase of population. The average enrollment, therefore, in the higher grades is unduly large as compared with that in the primary grades; for pupils attend more regularly in the higher than in the lower grades. Com-

---

[1] Table XVIII. *Influence of Death upon Duration of School Attendance*, p. 299. From the *Insurance Cyclopedia*, by C. Walford, Vol. II, pp. 528-32. Since the per cents derived from the English tables are computed upon the population of each age taken as a base, they must be recomputed (see column VI) upon the first grade as a base, to be usable in my tables. Column IV is taken from Table XVI. Column VI is derived from columns III and V.

paring the Milwaukee[1] with the Chicago tables, we may see that the same laws hold good in both cities as regards the dropping out of pupils.

Maximum Limit of Error. Let us now see whether we have in the inductive method as applied to Chicago the maximum limit of error. We have reduced the grade enrollments too much if anything; for the population-corrections, seven to thirteen per cent., included the increase from births as well as from immigration. But if the enrollments in Table XIV are made larger, the percentages in Table XV will be smaller and the per cents in Table XVI smaller. Hence so far as all except the first grade are concerned, the per cents are now as large as possible. But the first grade should be made smaller, if anything, because of double enrollment. This also would make the percentages in Tables XV and XVI smaller. So from both points of view the per cents that drop out are much too large, are the largest we can suppose possible, and, therefore, indicate the maximum limit, within which the truth lies.

Finally, if our enrollment in Table XIV be corrected not only for population but for double enrollment also, it is gratifying to find that we reach practically the same results as by our deductive method.[2] We thus find that the slow process of following a real class through grade after grade and making allowances for all possible errors only proves the close accuracy of the shorter deductive method.

FINAL COMPARISON OF RESULTS.

The next table[3] brings together for final comparison all the results thus far obtained, and shows that the conclusions of the deductive method occupy a middle position between the maxi-

---

[1] Table XIX. *Enrollment by Classes* (Milwaukee), p. 300.

Table XX. *Number Dropped out by End of Each Grade* (Milwaukee), p. 301.

Table XXI. *Per Cent. of First Grade Enrollment Dropped out by End of Each Grade* (Milwaukee), p. 302.

[2] Table XXII. *Per Cent. that Dropped out after Corrections for Double Enrollment*, p. 303. Compare with Table IV.

[3] Table XXIII. *Final Conclusions as to Per Cents that Drop out*, p. 304.

mum limit just reached, and the minimum limit as establishsd under the deductive method. The largest Milwaukee figures should not be given consideration, as they do not represent the enrollment of real classes, but "average membership."

Average Amount of Schooling per Pupil.—With these conclusions should be stated the number of grades reached by the average pupil. This is easily obtained from Table IX by dividing the total number of grade enrollments (one and one-half million) by the total number of pupils (one-half million). This gives approximately three grades to the average pupil. This is the least possible limit, because the first grade enrollment (one-half million) is more times too large than the total enrollment is, as was shown on page 267. If we use the figures of the same table after the correction for double enrollment, we get in the same way nearly four and one-half grades to the average pupil. This is the maximum estimate, because, as shown on the same page, the first grade is now reduced more times than it should be in comparison with the reduction of the grand total. There can be but little doubt, therefore, that the average pupil get less than four grades of schooling, and certainly he does not go beyond the primary grades.

In conclusion it should be clearly kept in mind just what our proposition is. It has not been proven, either as regards the average amount of schooling, or as regards the per cents that drop out at each grade, that these figures hold true outside of the two cities named, or even outside of the public schools in those cities; and when it is remembered that about one-third of the total school enrollment in each of these cities is in parochial and private schools,[1] it will be evident that we will need to bear this qualification in mind. Exactly formulated, our statement is this: "*Of the children that attend the public schools,* 32 per cent. drop out before reaching the second grade, 66 per cent. before reaching the fourth," and so on. That this statement, however, holds true of all schools, seems apparent from several lines of evidence that cannot be entered into here. One that falls within the scope of our inquiry, is the fact, that no

---

[1] Table XXIV. *Public and Private Schools of Chicago*, 1893-94, p. 305.

irregularities of enrollment are observable in the entire history of the public schools, such as might be caused by the opening or closing of private schools, and the transferring of pupils from public to parochial schools before confirmation, and from parochial to public schools at other ages. The inference, therefore, is that the pupils transferred are divided in about the same proportion amongst the grades in other schools, thus making no variations in our tables.

The St. Louis Statistics.—The evidence is still more conclusive that the proportions enrolled in these two cities are the normal proportions, not only in other cities of the United States, but even in rural districts and in other civilized countries. This was shown in the case of St. Louis by Dr. Harris in connection with his discussion of this subject.[1] His per cents are 33.3 for first grade, 18.6 for second grade and 19.9 for third, and so on and do not vary more than two per cent. in any grade from the Chicago norm, excepting in the third.

ENROLLMENT OF VARIOUS COUNTRIES.

	Primary Education.	Secondary Education.
	Per cent.	Per cent.
Chicago, 1893-94.............................	97.4	2.6
St. Louis, 1871-72..........................	97.4	2.6
United States, 1890-91 (public and private).....	97.4	2.6
United States, 1889-90 (public and private).....	97.5	2.5
United States, 1888-89 (public and private).....	98.1	1.9
United States, 1888-89 (public)................	96.1	3.9
United States, North Atlantic Division, 1890-91 (public)...........................	96.7	3.3
United States, South Atlantic Division, 1890-91 (public)	98.2	1.8
United States, South Central Division, 1890-91 (public)	98.4	1.6
United States, North Central Division, 1890-91 (public)	97.3	2.7
United States, Western Division, 1890-91(public).	97.0	3.0
Canada, 1890-91..............................	93.8	6.2
Great Britain and Ireland, 1890-91.............	96.2	3.8
Prussia, 1890-91..............................	94.3	5.7
France, 1890-91.	97.2	2.8
Netherlands. 1890-91	98.0	2.0
Norway, 1890-91..............................	93.6	6.4
Mexico, 1890-91..............................	96.0	4.0

---

[1] St. Louis Report for 1871-72, p. 25.
18

We cannot enter in this paper into a full discussion of the amount of schooling in other places, but it will be interesting to note in the foregoing list[1] that the per cent. in the high schools is quite uniform throughout all civilized countries.

The largest per cent. noted is that of Norway, 6.4, which is much larger than that of Chicago; while the smallest per cent. is found in some of our own southern states. No statistics have been found, through a somewhat extended search, that demonstrate the number dropped out in the lower grades, either at home, or abroad; but we may infer from the close correspondence everywhere as to secondary education that similar conditions would be found governing primary education. As is intimated further on, these conditions are fixed by economic and social influences which hold good in all countries.

Superintendent Smart's Conclusions.— It remains only to notice the few and imperfect calculations which have been made by others on the subject of this paper. In most cases there is no attempt at demonstration. I find, for instance, conclusions similar to those in this paper made by Ex-State-Supt. Charles T. Smart, of Ohio,[2] as follows: " The high schools, into which but about three per cent. of the pupils enrolled in the public schools ever enter, and from which less than one per cent. are graduated. . . . 50 per cent. of the youth enrolled in the public schools of the state do not attend school more than four years, and, under their existing circumstances, cannot attend more than five or six years; 75 per cent. stop attending school before entering the eighth year or grade, and 97 per cent. do not attend beyond the eighth year." (Pp. 472 and 473.) He adduces the same reason as suggested above: "A majority of the patrons of the public schools cannot do without the labor of their children, and therefore cannot give them time to attend school longer than five or six of the years devoted to primary instruction." (P. 473.)

London Estimates.— Similar testimony comes from the London School Board, England, as follows:[3]   " This leaves only 26.8

---

[1] *Report* of United States Bureau of Education 1890-91, pp. 40, 369-372.

[2] *Arena*, Vol. 10, p. 462 (September, 1894).

[3] From a paper read at a meeting of the London School Board by Sir

of the scholars for the upper standard, and justifies one of our inspectors in saying that, 'the charge of over instructing is wholly groundless; only 16.5 of the children receive instruction in specific subjects, the remainder, 83.5 being taught merely the three R's, and in the case of those above Standard I, a few simple facts relating to geography and grammar.'"

Dr. Wm. T. Harris's Method.— Dr. William T. Harris, United States Commissioner of Education, has for many years given thought to this subject. He was one of the earliest, apparently, to have a keen appreciation of the importance of determining the amount of schooling received by pupils; and has evidently based certain conclusions in his more famous papers of recent years, such as the determination of the course of study in his *Report of the Committee of Fifteen* upon the fact, that most pupils leave school with only a primary education. As long ago as 1872, while Superintendent of the St. Louis schools, he expressed a similar idea: "The average number of pupils in the lowest three years of the course was about 72 per cent. of the entire number enrolled. It was exactly the same for the year previous. The fact, that nearly three-fourths of all the pupils of the public schools are in the studies of the first three years or in the primary studies, exhibits the importance of making the instruction in those years the most efficient possible. On the supposition that a large percentage of our population will receive no other school education than what they get from the primary grades, pains have been taken to make the course of study not only disciplinary, but comprehensive in the subjects taught."[1] More positive was a statement in his first annual report as United States Commissioner of Education, in the following words:[2] "Six-sevenths of the population on arriving at the proper age for secondary education never receive it. Thirty out of thirty-one fail to receive higher education upon arriving at the proper age." The results reached in this paper are much the same.

Charles Reed: "Ten Years' Results of the London School-Board," *Journal of the Statistical Society*, Vol. 43, p. 676, December, 1880.

[1] St. Louis *Report* for 1871-72, p. 25.

[2] *Report* of the Commissioner of Education for the year 1888-89, p. xviii.

The method used by Dr. Harris in the reports named is much different from those of this paper. His words should be quoted in full: "If we divide the school population, which has been stated to form 34 per cent. of the total population, roughly into three classes, allowing for primary or elementary schools all between the ages of 6 and 13, inclusive, we shall set apart 20 per centum of the whole; the population aged from 14 to 17, inclusive, amounts to 8 per centum for secondary education; 6 per centum remains for the number aged 18 to 20, inclusive, for higher education. These percentages applied to the results shown by the statistics for the year 1889 give us the following ratios:

".For the 12,000,000 of school age for elementary instruction there were actually enrolled in public and private schools 12,931,259, or an excess of nearly 1,000,000. For the 4,750,000 of school age for secondary instruction there were actually enrolled only 668,461, or less than one-seventh of the youth of age for that grade of work. Of the 4,000,000 of right age for higher education there were enrolled only 126,854, or less than one-thirtieth of the quota."

This is one of the methods at first attempted in this investigation. It was despaired of, however, for the ages actually found in the city schools varied so greatly from Dr. Harris's premises as to make it nearly useless. Thus, while he takes the years from fourteen to seventeen as the high school age, the pupils actually in the high school in 1893–94 were of the following ages:[1]

From ten to eleven years of age...2
From eleven to twelve years of age......................................6
From twelve to thirteen years of age...................................43
From thirteen to fourteen years of age................................261
From fourteen to fifteen years of age.................................809
From fifteen to sixteen years of age................................1,395
From sixteen to seventeen years of age..............................1,471
Over seventeen years of age...2,202

· Even if this method were sufficient in regard to secondary education or elementary education, as a whole, it would be manifestly insufficient to show the number dropping out of *each grade.*

---

[1] *Report* of the Board, 1894, p. 204.

In a later report[1] the results of Dr. Harris seem to be somewhat different from my own, but the difference may be apparent rather than real. What he really reaches in this chapter is not the number or per cent. that withdraws at each grade, but the average age at which pupils withdraw. He quotes with approval Prof. C. M. Woodward's method, which results in an age at withdrawal of about $13\frac{1}{2}$ years for the average pupil. Since the latter enters school at $7\frac{1}{2}$ years of age, this would give him only five years of schooling, which may be entirely consistent with the $3\frac{1}{2}$ or 4 grades which the average pupil attends, as shown by my method; for as has already been shown, more than one-half of the pupils go a second year to the first grade alone, and the average required considerably over one year each in the second and third grades.[2]

Other Estimates.—The estimates most widely differing from those in this paper which I have found are those of Superintendents White and Lane. Those of the former seem so unreasonable, in the absence of adequate information as to the method employed in deducing them, that they may be simply inserted at this point without further discussion.[3]

Estimates of the Number that do not go Beyond the Grades Named.

Grades.	Supt. Lane.	Supt. White.	This paper.
First.......................................	10 1	10	32.2
Second.....................................	19.7	15	50.6
Third......................................	34.3	25	66.1
Fourth.....................................	39.0	40	77 6
Fifth	51.6	50	86.2
Sixth......................................	62.9	60	91.8
Seventh....................................	71.2	70	95.2
Eighth.....................................	....	85	97.4
Ninth......................................	....	90	98.6
Tenth......................................	....	94	99.3
Eleventh...................................	....	95	99.7
Twelfth....................................	....	100	100.0

[1] *Report* of the Commissioner of Education for the year 1891–92, Vol. I, Chap. XIV. "The Age of Withdrawal from the Public Schools."

[2] See p. 266, *supra*, on promotions.

[3] Superintendent White's estimates are found in his *Promotions and Examinations*, quoted by J. N. Patrick, *Elements of Pedagogics*, p.

Superintendent Lane's results expressed in the same terms
as those used in this paper, would give us only 10 per cent.
that drop out at the first grade, 15 per cent. at the second,
and so forth. There are two errors iu his method so fundamental and enormous as to make it valueless: the first is that
he has made no correction for the increase of the higher grades
through immigration and annexation; the second is that he has
not taken the real enrollment numbers, as has been done in this
paper, but has taken the average daily membership of the first
grade and has traced the progress of this fictitious class through
the higher grades, also in terms of average daily membership.
The great uncertainty of his method appears at once upon applying it to the Milwaukee daily membership, as has been done
in Tables V to VII (pp. 286-8). The result here must be very
unwelcome to Mr. Lane, for it shows that his method gives
almost exactly the same numbers dropping out of each grade
that this paper does.

In our survey of the printed material of the subject, it is
evident that no sufficient reason has been found to modify the
conclusions of this paper. Even the most different estimates,
made by people of various degrees of familiarity with the subject, all agree that from 40 to 80 per cent. never get into the
grammar grades, and that from 85 to 95 per cent. never reach the
high school. Methods and estimates are most at variance below
the grammar grades, especially in the first and second grades.
It might be objected that compulsory education laws result in
a longer attendance at school than is apparent in these statistics. There are two sufficient answers to this claim: first, it is
not enforced, as the superintendent of the Chicago schools has
repeatedly said in his reports;[1] in the second place, if enforced
it would not necessarily carry the pupil beyond the third grade.
A simple computation will show that if he be compelled to

---

171. Superintendent Lane's figures are obtained by subtraction from the
table on page 35 of the *Annual Report* of the Board of Education, Chicago, for 1897. Superintendent Lane was moved by my tables to this
attempt to reach different conclusions. His method was pre-figured in a
personal letter written me May 13, 1895.

[1] *Report* of the Board, 1895, p. 48, for example.

attend only four months in a year for seven years, he receives a total schooling of 28 months, which is a little less than three grades — even if we disregard the fact that he will have to take the work of some term a second time over, and probably of more than one term, because of the long intervals between his terms of attendance.

CAUSES AND REMEDIES.

It would be interesting to make a thorough investigation of the causes that account for this small amount of schooling on the part of the average pupil; in fact, it is absolutely necessary to secure a correct diagnosis of the case before adequate remedies can be applied. It is rather a thankless task, however, for everybody considers himself able to point out the real difficulty; although there should be no need, before a scientific association, for saying that only the judgment of the specialist is of much value. It is a difficult problem in itself and is not the problem of this paper; therefore only a few brief suggestions have been added by request.

The actions of pupils, like those of other people, are governed by their interests. To a great extent they do not like the school or the teacher, or they like other things better. But the controlling motive is to do as their parents wish or command. Hence we must determine what causes the attitude of parents in regard to sending their children to school. I answer without hesitation that the chief factors are economic conditions. Too many either cannot support their children as they desire, or cannot spare them through a longer period of schooling; others simply wish the wages their children may earn more than they wish their education. A few are opposed to higher education. Others humor their children in their dislike of school. But a most important motive still remains, namely, the wish to live in accordance with the social demands of the community or to obey the law which the community makes.

So we finally must ascertain the causes of the social sentiment which may lead as one result to compulsory education laws. An analysis would reduce this sentiment to ideas concerning the safety of the state and the need of education —

ideas that are inherited rather than reached through rational conviction, ideas that are a survival of the fittest. Dr. Harris rationally voices this thought in his relating education to the "needs of civilization."

Which, now, are the chief causes of early withdrawal from school? Is not the greatest cause the economic? If so, the remedy is to be found in improving the economic conditions, and we know that this is not easily done. The next best remedy is to educate parents and the community to the need of more schooling; but this is a slow process. The most direct remedy is the enactment and enforcement of a good compulsory education law. This may, in turn, require a brief term of education on the part of the law makers and the makers of public opinion. But it must be recognized that another great deficiency is the failure on the part of the teacher to make school work as interesting as it should be. The remedy in this case is to educate better the teachers and to exercise more care in the selection of them. One further suggestion may be made. Since the child's education is not now compulsory before the age of seven, add a year or two before that in the compulsory education law, and provide kindergartens for the earlier work.

SUMMARY.

The chief proposition which has been elaborated in the foregoing pages may be stated as follows: Of all that enter the public schools of Chicago and Milwaukee,

(1) About one-third go no further than the first grade;

(2) About one-half go no further than the second grade;

(3) About two-thirds go no further than the third grade;

(4) About three-fouths go no further than the fourth grade;

(5) About nine-tenths go only half way through the twelve grades;

(6) About ninety-seven in every hundred drop out before reaching the High School;

(7) Only three in every thousand finish the entire course.

Or, more exactly, the following per cents drop out at each grade:

Grade,	1	2	3	4	5	6	7	8	9	10	11.
Per cent.,	32	51	66	78	86	92	95	97	98.6	99.3	99.7.

Another line of argument leads to the conclusion that the schooling of the average pupil does not embrace more than three grades. Although the evidence is far from sufficient, it further appears probable that these statements hold true of the average citizen of the United States wherever found.

TABLE I.— *Enrollment of Public Schools.*—Chicago.

FIFTEEN YEARS.

GRADE.	For the School Year Ending in —														
	1880.	1881.	1882.	1883.	1884.	1885.	1886.	1887.	1888.	1889.	1890.	1891.	1892.	1893.	1894.
First	18,572	20,459	23,795	25,621	26,890	28,288	25,444	27,954	29,479	29,610	41,502	43,601	46,404	47,121	54,935
Second	10,813	11,409	12,839	13,261	13,783	15,007	15,838	16,627	17,165	17,772	24,052	26,653	27,703	29,425	30,615
Third	10,538	10,395	10,770	11,358	11,567	11,512	12,227	12,971	13,410	14,579	21,351	21,602	23,814	25,721	27,267
Fourth	7,231	7,968	8,044	7,833	8,507	8,511	8,974	9,015	9,981	10,631	15,423	18,049	18,348	19,969	22,888
Total Primary	47,174	50,231	55,448	58,073	60,747	63,318	65,483	66,567	70,035	72,592	102,418	109,908	116,269	122,130	135,735
Fifth	4,739	5,411	5,207	5,097	5,938	6,637	6,971	7,037	7,118	7,703	11,943	13,191	14,877	16,382	17,430
Sixth	3,291	3,194	3,455	3,678	3,796	3,933	4,433	4,632	5,064	5,244	8,147	8,444	10,154	11,035	12,183
Seventh	1,906	2,000	1,929	2,181	2,532	2,181	2,601	2,824	3,123	3,420	5,028	5,871	6,027	6,301	7,866
Eighth	923	1,016	1,157	1,091	1,388	1,452	1,503	1,707	1,903	2,144	3,714	4,202	4,679	4,985	5,670
Total Grammar	10,859	11,621	11,748	12,950	13,714	14,203	15,511	16,200	17,208	18,511	28,832	31,708	35,737	38,703	43,149
Ninth	772	550	671	711	743	827	946	891	982	1,112	1,960	2,362	2,614	2,627	2,699
Tenth	483	448	362	414	424	432	547	610	602	646	1,107	1,326	1,499	1,591	1,760
Eleventh	91	169	211	176	212	236	255	378	424	448	653	810	941	1,024	1,050
Twelfth	114	69	133	135	156	136	171	208	278	337	480	483	585	697	707
Total High School	1,460	1,236	1,377	1,436	1,535	1,701	1,959	2,087	2,286	2,543	4,200	4,981	5,639	5,939	6,165
Corrected totals	59,493	63,088	68,573	72,459	75,996	79,222	82,953	84,854	89,529	93,646	135,450	146,597	157,645	166,781	185,049
Post-graduate	....	....	....	....	....	....	....	....	....	....	....	13	4	24	24
Deaf mutes and waifs	....	....	....	....	....	....	....	....	....	....	....	88	94	90	*285
Ungraded	69	53	41	50	48	54	69	48	49	91	91	53	....	....	....
Published totals	59,562	63,141	68,614	72,509	76,044	79,276	83,022	84,902	89,578	93,737	135,541	146,751	157,743	166,895	185,358

*Including 205 in House of Correction.

TABLE II.— *Average Daily Membership.*—Chicago, 1875-76 to 1880-81.

GRADE.	FOR THE SCHOOL YEAR ENDING IN —					
	1876.	1877.	1878.	1879.	1880.	1881.
First	8,936	10,242.8	10,619.7	11,472.4	11,155.0	11,788.3
Second	8,857	8,133.1	8,051.2	8,302.5	8,779.6	9,147.3
Third	6,672	7,160.4	7,843.4	8.402.7	8,278.3	8,664.9
Fourth	4,648	5,003.1	5,465.6	5,329.2	6,255.9	6,646.8
Total Primary..........	29,113	30,539.4	31,989.9	33,504.8	34,468.8	36,247.3
Fifth	3,089	2,853.9	3,223.8	3,933.4	4,242.7	4,689.0
Sixth.............................	2,290	2,460.2	2,359.2	2,501.4	2,659.0	2,796.3
Seventh	1,586	1,486.9	1,675.9	1,654.3	1,728.5	1,821.0
Eighth	994	867.9	988.6	835.7	768.6	898.7
Total Grammar.........	7,959	7,668.9	8,247.4	8,924.8	9,398.8	10,205.0
Ninth	550.5	674.3	743.2	644.0	582.5	477.5
Tenth	239.8	396.2	441.0	465.6	420.1	355.0
Eleventh	76.2	56.9	91.7	111.4	71.3	146.9
Twelfth	63.7	50.5	56.1	66.6	105.1	63.7
Total High School......	917.8	1,177.9	1,332.0	1,287.6	1,179.0	1,043.1
Totals..................	37,989.8	39,386.2	41,569.3	43,717.2	45,075.9	47,523.0

TABLE III.— Per Cent. of Enrollment in each Grade.—Chicago.

GRADE.	1880.	1881.	1882.	1883.	1884.	1885.	1886.	1887.	1888.	1889.	1890.	1891.	1892.	1893.	1894.	Av. 15 years.
First	31.12	32.43	34.70	35.36	35.38	35.62	34.23	32.95	32.93	31.61	30.68	29.74	29.43	28.26	29.68	32.28
Second	18.17	18.00	18.72	18.31	18.17	19.02	19.14	19.50	19.06	18.93	17.76	18.11	17.58	17.65	16.56	18.32
Third	17.78	16.48	15.71	15.68	15.22	14.55	14.74	15.29	15.09	15.62	15.78	14.87	15.11	15.42	14.74	15.54
Fourth	12.15	12.62	11.73	10.79	11.20	10.74	10.80	10.63	11.15	11.35	11.39	12.29	11.65	11.91	12.37	11.52
Fifth	7.99	8.53	7.60	8.28	7.88	8.37	8.40	8.29	7.94	8.23	8.84	8.99	9.44	9.82	9.42	8.54
Sixth	5.53	5.06	5.04	5.08	4.99	4.96	5.34	5.45	5.66	5.59	6.00	5.76	6.49	6.62	6.59	5.60
Seventh	3.25	3.17	2.80	3.01	3.33	2.75	3.14	3.33	3.49	3.64	3.72	4.00	3.82	3.78	4.25	3.42
Eighth	1.56	1.61	1.69	1.51	1.84	1.83	1.81	2.01	2.13	2.29	2.75	2.86	2.97	2.99	3.06	2.19
Ninth	1.30	.87	.98	.98	.97	1.05	1.11	1.05	1.10	1.19	1.44	1.61	1.66	1.58	1.46	1.21
Tenth	.81	.71	.53	.57	.55	.61	.66	.74	.67	.68	.81	.90	.94	.95	.92	.72
Eleventh	.15	.27	.31	.24	.27	.30	.35	.44	.48	.47	.48	.55	.60	.61	.57	.40
Twelfth	.19	.11	.19	.19	.20	.20	.20	.23	.30	.35	.35	.32	.31	.41	.38	.26
Totals	100.00	100.00	100.00	100.00	100.00	100.00	100.00	100.00	100.00	100.00	100.00	100.00	100.00	100.00	100.00	100.00

TABLE IV.— *Per Cent. of Pupils that do not go beyond the Grade Named.*—Chicago.

GRADE.	FOR THE SCHOOL YEAR ENDING IN—															Av. 15 yrs.
	1880.	1881.	1882.	1883.	1884.	1885.	1886.	1887.	1888.	1889.	1890.	1891.	1892.	1893.	1894.	
First	31.12	32.43	31.70	35.36	35.38	35.62	34.28	32.95	32.93	31.61	30.68	29.74	29.43	28.26	29.68	32.28
Second	49.20	50.52	53.42	53.67	53.55	51.64	53.42	52.54	51.99	50.?9	48.44	47.85	47.01	45.91	46.24	50.60
Third	67.07	67.00	69.13	69.35	68.77	69.19	63.16	67.83	67.08	66.21	64.22	62.72	62.12	61.33	60.98	66.14
Fourth	79.22	79.62	80.86	80.14	79.97	79.93	79.96	78.46	78.23	77.56	75.61	75.01	73.77	73.24	73.35	77.66
Fifth	87.21	88.20	88.46	88.42	87.85	88.30	88.36	86.75	86.17	85.79	84.45	84.00	83.21	83.06	82.77	86.20
Sixth	92.74	93.26	93.50	93.50	92.84	93.26	93.70	92.20	91.83	91.38	90.45	89.76	89.70	89.68	89.36	91.80
Seventh	96.99	96.43	96.30	96.51	96.17	86.01	96.94	95.53	95.32	95.02	91.17	93.76	93.52	93.46	93.61	95.22
Eighth	97.55	98.04	97.99	98.02	98.01	97.84	97.65	97.54	97.45	97.31	96.92	96.62	96.49	96.45	96.67	97.41
Ninth	98.85	98.91	98.97	99.00	98.98	98.89	98.79	98.59	98.55	98.50	98.36	98.23	98.15	98.03	98.13	98.62
Tenth	99.66	99.62	99.50	99.57	99.53	99.50	99.45	99.33	99.22	99.18	99.17	99.13	99.09	98.98	99.05	99.34
Eleventh	99.81	99.89	99.81	99.81	99.80	99.80	99.80	99.77	99.70	99.65	99.65	99.68	99.69	99.59	99.62	99.74
Twelfth	100.00	100.00	100.00	100.00	100.00	100.00	100.00	100.00	100.00	100.00	100.00	100.00	100.00	100.00	100.00	100.00

TABLE V.—Per Cent. of Enrollment in Each Grade.—Milwaukee.

GRADE.	For the School Year Ending in—																	
	1890.	1881.	1882.	1883.	1884.	1885.	1886.	1887.	1888.	1889.	1890.	1891.	1892.	1893.	1894.	1895.	1896.	1897.
Kindergarten	......	......	......	......	......	4	6	7	8	10	11	10	11	11	11	11	11	11
First	39	37	40	40	41	37	35	36	33	34	34	35	33	33	29	27	26	25
Second	16	16	15	15	15	15	16	16	16	14	15	15	16	14	15	14	14	14
Third	16	17	15	14	14	15	14	13	14	13	12	12	12	13	13	13	12	13
Fourth	13	12	12	12	11	11	11	11	11	11	10	10	10	10	11	11	11	11
Fifth	7	9	9	9	8	7	8	7	8	8	8	7	7	7	8	9	9	9
Sixth	4	4	5	5	6	5	5	5	5	5	5	6	5	5	6	7	8	7
Seventh	3	3	2	3	3	4	3	3	3	3	3	3	4	4	4	5	5	5
Eighth	2	2	2	2	2	2	2	2	2	2	2	2	2	3	3	3	4	4

Table VI.—*Per Cent. of Enrollment in Each Grade with Corrections for Kindergarten and High School.*— Milwaukee.

GRADE.	For the School Year Ending in—																		Average 18 years.
	1880.	1881.	1882.	1883.	1884.	1885.	1886.	1887.	1888.	1889.	1890.	1891.	1892.	1893.	1894.	1895.	1896.	1897.	
First	38.2	36.2	39.2	39.2	40.3	37.9	36.3	37.8	35.0	36.8	36.9	37.8	36.0	35.9	31.5	29.0	27.9	26.9	34.9
Second	15.7	15.7	14.7	14.7	14.7	13.4	16.6	16.7	16.9	15.2	16.3	16.2	17.5	15.3	16.3	15.1	15.1	15.1	15.8
Third	15.7	16.7	14.7	13.7	13.8	15.4	14.5	13.7	14.8	14.1	13.0	13.0	13.1	14.2	14.1	14.0	12.9	14.0	14.2
Fourth	12.7	11.7	11.7	11.8	10.8	11.2	11.5	11.5	11.7	11.9	10.8	10.8	11.0	10.9	11.9	11.9	11.8	11.9	11.5
Fifth	6.9	8.7	8.8	8.9	7.9	7.2	8.4	7.3	8.5	8.7	8.6	7.6	7.7	7.6	8.7	9.7	9.7	9.9	9.0
Sixth	3.9	3.9	4.9	4.9	5.9	5.1	5.2	5.4	5.3	5.4	5.4	6.5	5.5	5.5	6.6	7.6	8.6	7.6	5.7
Seventh	2.9	2.9	2.0	3.0	2.9	4.1	3.2	3.2	3.2	3.3	3.2	3.3	4.4	4.4	4.3	5.4	5.4	5.4	3.7
Eighth	2.0	2.0	2.0	2.0	2.0	2.1	2.2	2.1	2.1	2.2	2.2	2.2	2.2	3.3	3.3	3.2	4.3	4.3	2.5
High School	2.0	2.2	2.0	1.8	1.7	1.6	2.1	2.3	2.5	2.4	2.6	2.6	2.6	2.9	3.3	4.1	4.3	4.9	2.7

TABLE VII.—*Per Cent. of Pupils that do not go beyond the Grade Named.*—Milwaukee.

GRADE.	For the School Year Ending in—																		Av.
	1880	1881	1882	1883	1884	1885	1886	1887	1888	1889	1890	1891	1892	1893	1894	1895	1896	1897	
First	38.2	36.2	39.2	39.2	40.3	37.9	36.3	37.8	35.0	36.8	36.9	37.8	36.0	35.9	31.5	29.0	27.9	26.9	34.9
Second	53.9	51.0	53.9	53.9	55.0	53.3	52.9	51.5	51.9	52.0	53.2	54.0	53.5	51.2	47.3	44.1	43.0	42.0	50.7
Third	69.6	68.6	68.6	67.6	68.8	68.7	67.4	68.2	66.7	66.1	66.2	67.0	66.6	63.6	61.9	58.1	55.9	56.0	64.9
Fourth	82.3	80.3	80.3	79.4	79.6	79.9	78.9	79.7	78.4	78.0	77.0	77.8	77.6	76.3	73.8	70.0	67.7	67.9	76.4
Fifth	89.2	89.0	89.1	88.3	87.5	87.1	87.3	87.0	86.9	86.7	85.6	85.4	85.3	83.9	82.5	79.7	77.4	77.8	85.4
Sixth	93.1	92.9	91.0	93.2	93.4	92.3	92.5	92.4	92.2	92.1	92.0	91.9	90.8	89.4	89.1	87.3	86.0	85.4	91.1
Seventh	96.0	95.8	96.0	96.2	96.3	96.3	95.7	95.6	95.1	95.4	95.2	95.2	95.2	93.8	93.4	92.7	91.4	90.8	94.5
Eighth	98.0	97.8	98.0	98.2	98.3	98.4	97.9	97.7	97.5	97.6	97.4	97.4	97.4	97.1	96.7	95.9	95.7	95.1	97.3
High School	100.0	100.0	100.0	100.0	100.0	100.0	100.0	100.0	100.0	100.0	100.0	100.0	100.0	100.0	100.0	100.0	100.0	100.0	100.0

TABLE VIII.—*Number of Pupils Promoted.*—Chicago.

GRADE TO WHICH PROMOTED.	FOR THE SCHOOL YEAR ENDING IN—										
	1884	1885	1886	1887	1888	1889	1890	1891	1892	1893	1894
Second	9,238	10,101	10,317	10,395	11,912	13,624	20,187	21,371	22,980	25,506	26,550
Third	7,684	8,642	9,109	9,530	10,706	12,491	17,530	19,173	20,616	22,025	24,052
Fourth	6,532	7,440	7,791	8,117	9,057	10,268	15,831	16,207	17,796	19,988	21,500
Fifth	4,953	5,571	6,056	5,912	7,080	8,184	12,057	13,121	14,165	15,515	18,273
Sixth	3,147	3,928	4,256	4,175	4,814	5,733	8,616	9,796	10,478	11,666	13,715
Seventh	2,025	2,520	2,880	2,902	3,328	3,768	6,086	6,348	7,724	8,199	9,376
Eighth	1,509	1,515	1,758	1,928	2,112	2,717	4,021	4,651	4,900	5,541	6,493
High School	1,183	1,227	1,285	1,389	1,654	1,924	3,133	3,458	3,387	4,046	4,928

TABLE IX.— *True or Entrance Enrollment.*—Chicago.

GRADE.	Enrollment (15 years.)	Per cent. not promoted.	Corrected enrollment.	PER CENT. DROPPED.	
				In each grade.	By end of each grade.
First......................	492,738	45	339,819	26.7	27
Second....................	282,992	33	212,776	16.7	43
Third	239,135	25	187,308	14.7	58
Fourth....................	181,272	10	164,792	12.9	71
Fifth......................	136,631	....	136,631	10.7	82
Sixth...	90,683	....	90,683	7.2	89
Seventh...................	55,793	....	55,793	4.4	93
Eighth....................	37,547	....	37,547	3.0	96
Ninth.....................	20,467	....	20,467	1.7	98
Tenth.....................	12,240	....	12,240	1.0	99
Eleventh..................	7,118	....	7,118	.6	99.6
Twelfth................. ...	4,719	....	4,719	.4	100
Totals	1,561,335	....	1,270,893	100.0	....

TABLE X.—*Method of Obtaining Population Corrections.* (Illustrated for the class entering in 1879-80.)

YEAR.	Census.	Increase over 1880.	Per cent. of increase.[1]	INCREMENTS.[1]		Population corrections	Grades.
				Actual.	Estimated.		
1880....	491,516	0	0	0	0	0	First.
1881....	....	....	....	....	7.0	7.0	Second.
1882....	560,693	69,177	14.0	14.0	7.0	14.0	Third.
1883....	....	....	....	....	7.0	21.0	Fourth
1884....	629,985	138,469	28.1	14.1	7.1	28.1	Fifth.
1885....	....	....	....	....	7.3	35.4	Sixth.
1886....	703,817	212,301	43.1	15.0	7.7	43.1	Seventh.
1887....	....	....	....	....	9.0	52.1	Eighth.
1888....	802,651	311,135	63.3	20.2	11.2	63.3	Ninth.
1889....	....	....	....	....	11.5	74.8	Tenth.
1890....	1,208,669	717,153	145.9	82.6	(59.1)[2] 12.0	145.9	Eleventh.
1891....	....	....	....	....	(21.3)[2] 12.5	179.7	Twelfth.
1892...	1,438,010	946,494	192.7	46.8	13.0	192.7	....
1893....	....	....	....	....	13.0	205.7	....
1894....	1,567,727	1,076,034	218.9	26.2	13.2	218.9	....

[1] Computed on population of 1890.

[2] The real increments very large, on account of annexed districts in 1890 and 1891; the per cents. given in parenthesis would have been normal increments, as is evident from the rest.

TABLE XI.—*Population Corrections.*

(Numbers not in bold type are estimated.)

For Enrollment in—	For the Class Entering in—														
	1879-80	1880-81	1881-82	1882-83	1883-84	1884-85	1885-86	1886-87	1887-88	1888-89	1889-90	1890-91	1891-92	1892-93	1893-94
1879-90	0.														
1880-81	7.0	0.													
1881-82	14.0	6.5	0.												
1882-93	21.0	13.0	6.0	0.											
1883-84	28.1	19.6	12.3	6 0	0.										
1884-85	35.4	26.4	18.8	12.0	5.5	0.									
1885-86	43.1	33.6	25.7	18.4	11.5	5.5	0.								
1886-87	52.1	42.1	33.7	26.1	19.0	12.8	7.0	0.							
1887-88	63.3	52.3	43.1	35.1	27.4	20.8	14.4	7.0	0.						
1888-89	74.8	63.1	53.1	44.4	36.2	29.3	22.4	14.2	5.5	0.					
1889-90	145.9	128.4	115.5	102.2	90.9	81.1	71.7	61.7	50.5	42.2	0.				
1890-91	179.7	160.1	145.4	130.9	118.8	107.3	79.7	85.5	72.2	59.7	13.9	0.			
1891-92	192.7	172.2	156.4	141.3	128.5	116.5	104.3	93.5	79.2	65.7	18.9	4.5	0.		
1892-93	205.7	184.4	167.9	152.0	138.5	126.2	113.3	101.5	86.2	71.8	24.1	9.3	4.4	0.	
1893-94	218.9	196.8	179.6	163.0	148.9	136.0	122.6	109.8	93.5	78.1	29.5	14.3	8.9	8.9	0.

TABLE XII.— *Estimated Per Cents of Increase of Population.*

FOR THE CLASS ENTERING IN—

ENROLLMENT.	1879-80	1880-81	1881-82	1882-83	1883-84	1884-85	1885-86	1886-87	1887-88	1888-89	1889-90	1890-91	1891-92	1892-93	1893-94
1879-80	0.														
1880-81	7.0	0.													
1881-82	7.0	6.5	0.												
1882-83	7.0	6.5	6.0	0.											
1883-84	7.1	6.6	6.3	6.0	0.										
1884-85	7.3	6.8	6.5	6.0	5.5	0.									
1885-86	7.7	7.2	6.9	6.4	6.0	5.5	0.								
1886-87	9.0	8.5	8.0	7.7	7.5	7.3	7.0	0.							
1887-88	11.2	10.2	9.4	9.0	8.4	8.0	7.4	7.0	0.						
1888-89	11.5	10.8	10.0	9.3	8.3	8.5	8.0	7.2	5.5	0.					
1889-90	{39.1 / 12.0}	{44.9 / 11.3}	{61.9 / 10.5}	{44.0 / 9.9}	{45.6 / 9.2}	{43.0 / 8.8}	{41.3 / 8.0}	{40.8 / 7.5}	{39.6 / 5.5}	{37.0 / 5.2}	0.				
1890-91	{21.3 / 12.5}	{20.0 / 11.7}	{16.9 / 11.0}	{16.5 / 10.2}	{16.4 / 9.5}	{17.0 / 9.2}	{16.1 / 8.5}	{16.0 / 7.8}	{16.2 / 6.5}	{12.0 / 5.5}	{8.9 / 5.0}	0.			
1891-92	13.0	12.1	11.0	10.4	9.7	9.4	8.5	8.0	7.0	6.0	5.0	4.5	0.		
1892-93	13.0	12.2	11.5	10.7	10.0	9.5	9.0	8.0	7.0	6.1	5.2	4.8	4.4	0.	
1893-94	13.2	12.4	11.7	11.0	10.4	9.8	9.3	8.3	7.3	6.3	5.4	5.0	4.5	4.0	0.

TABLE XIII.—*Enrollment by Classes.*—Chicago. Fifteen Years.

GRADE.	CLASS ENTERING IN THE YEAR—														
	1879-80	1880-81	1881-82	1882-83	1883-84	1884-85	1885-86	1886-87	1887-88	1888-89	1889-90	1890-91	1891-92	1892-93	1893-94
First	18,572	20,459	23,795	25,621	26,890	23,288	28,444	27,954	29,479	29,610	41,562	43,604	46,404	47,121	54,935
Second	11,400	12,839	13,281	13,783	15,067	15,838	16,627	17,165	17,772	24,052	26,633	27,703	29,455	30,645	
Third	10,770	11,358	11,567	11,512	12,227	12,971	13,410	14,579	21,381	21,602	23,811	25,724	27,267		
Fourth	7,833	8,507	8,511	8,974	9,015	9,981	10,631	15,423	18,049	18,318	19,969	22,888			
Fifth	5,988	6,637	6,971	7,037	7,118	7,703	11,943	13,191	14,877	16,382	17,430				
Sixth	3,933	4,433	4,632	5,064	5,234	8,147	8,444	10,154	11,035	12,183					
Seventh	2,604	2,821	3,123	3,120	5,023	5,871	6,027	6,310	7,866						
Eighth	1,707	1,903	2,144	3,714	4,202	4,679	4,985	5,670							
Ninth	982	1,112	1,960	2,362	2,614	2,627	2,699								
Tenth	646	1,107	1,326	1,439	1,591	1,709									
Eleventh	653	810	941	1,024	1,030										
Twelfth	438	595	697	707											

TABLE XIV.—*Corrected Enrollment by Classes.*—Chicago.

GRADE.	CLASS ENTERING IN THE YEAR—														
	1879-80	1880-81	1881-82	1882-83	1883-84	1884-85	1885-86	1886-87	1887-88	1888-89	1889-90	1890-91	1891-92	1892-93	1893-94
First	18,572	20,459	23,795	25,621	26,890	28,288	28,444	27,954	29,479	29,610	41,562	43,604	46,401	47,121	54,935
Second	10,662	12,065	12,509	13,002	14,281	15,012	15,539	16,042	16,845	16,914	21,400	26,510	28,184	28,141	......
Third	9,447	10,051	10,300	10,278	10,965	11,409	11,722	12,766	14,206	13,526	20,028	23,535	25,038	......	......
Fourth	6,475	7,112	7,164	7,479	7,575	8,262	8,685	9,538	10,481	11,073	16,010	20,024	......	......	......
Fifth	4,678	5,250	5,544	5,572	5,587	5,957	6,955	7,111	8,313	9,535	13,459	......	......	......	......
Sixth	2,908	3,318	3,464	3,748	3,850	4,493	4,698	5,247	5,925	6,840	......	......	......	......	......
Seventh	1,821	2,198	2,181	2,969	2,634	2,832	2,950	3,127	4,065	......	......	......	......	......	......
Eighth	1,123	1,249	1,400	1,836	1,920	2,159	2,337	2,702	......	......	......	......	......	......	......
Ninth	601	1,682	909	1,023	1,144	1,155	1,212	......	......	......	......	......	......	......	......
Tenth	370	479	510	617	666	724	......	......	......	......	......	......	......	......	......
Eleventh	224	311	367	406	422	......	......	......	......	......	......	......	......	......	......
Twelfth	173	218	260	288	......	......	......	......	......	......	......	......	......	......	......

TABLE XV.—*Number Dropped Out by End of Each Grade.*—Chicago.

GRADE.	CLASS ENDING IN THE YEAR—													
	1879-80	1880-81	1881-82	1882-83	1883-84	1884-85	1885-86	1886-87	1887-88	1888-89	1889-90	1890-91	1891-92	1892-93
First	7,910	8,404	11,296	12,619	12,637	13,276	12,905	11,912	12,634	12,696	18,153	17,094	18,220	18,980
Second	9,125	10,408	13,495	15,343	15,825	16,777	16,722	15,188	15,273	16,084	21,534	20,069	21,366	......
Third	12,097	13,347	16,631	18,142	19,315	20,026	19,759	18,416	18,908	18,537	25,552	23,580	......	......
Fourth	13,394	15,209	18,251	20,049	21,303	22,331	21,489	20,843	21,166	20,075	28,103	......	......	......
Fifth	15,064	17,141	20,331	21,873	23,047	23,795	23,746	22,707	23,554	22,770	......	......	......	......
Sixth	16,751	18,261	21,614	23,252	24,257	25,456	25,494	24,827	25,414	......	......	......	......	......
Seventh	17,449	19,210	22,395	23,785	24,970	26,129	26,107	25,252	......	......	......	......	......	......
Eighth	17,971	19,777	22,886	24,598	25,746	27,133	27,232	......	......	......	......	......	......	......
Ninth	18,292	19,980	23,255	25,004	26,224	27,564	......	......	......	......	......	......	......	......
Tenth	18,348	20,148	23,428	25,215	26,468	......	......	......	......	......	......	......	......	......
Eleventh	18,399	20,241	23,535	25,353	......	......	......	......	......	......	......	......	......	......
Twelfth	18,572	20,459	23,795	25,621	......	......	......	......	......	......	......	......	......	......

TABLE XVI.—*Per Cent. of First Grade Enrollment Dropped Out by End of Each Grade.*—Chicago.

GRADE.	CLASS ENTERING IN THE YEAR—														Average.
	1879-80	1880-81	1881-82	1882-83	1883-84	1884-85	1885-86	1886-87	1887-88	1888-89	1889-90	1890-91	1891-92	1892-93	
First	42.59	41.02	49.11	49.25	43.53	46.93	45.00	42.61	40.82	42.89	43.67	39.20	39.26	40.27	43.29
Second	49.13	50.87	58.40	59.92	58.85	58.93	58.79	54.43	51.81	54.32	51.83	46.02	46.04	......	53.79
Third	65.13	65.23	69.85	70.79	72.70	70.79	69.46	64.09	64.44	62.67	61.23	54.08	......	......	65.87
Fourth	74.81	74.39	76.70	78.25	79.21	77.81	75.56	74.56	71.30	67.76	67.61	......	......	......	74.42
Fifth	84.33	83.53	85.45	85.80	85.77	84.13	83.83	81.27	79.90	76.86	......	......	......	......	83.08
Sixth	90.19	90.55	90.84	90.75	90.20	89.95	89.62	89.85	92.82	......	......	......	......	......	89.07
Seventh	93.89	93.75	94.12	92.83	92.86	92.38	91.78	90.32	......	......	......	......	......	......	92.85
Eighth	96.76	96.51	96.18	96.00	95.91	96.31	95.73	......	......	......	......	......	......	......	96.20
Ninth	97.00	97.52	97.73	97.59	97.52	97.43	......	......	......	......	......	......	......	......	97.48
Tenth	98.79	98.31	98.47	98.41	98.43	......	......	......	......	......	......	......	......	......	98.48
Eleventh	99.67	98.77	98.90	98.91	......	......	......	......	......	......	......	......	......	......	99.06
Twelfth	100.00	100.00	100.00	100.00	......	......	......	......	......	......	......	......	......	......	100.00

TABLE XVII.— *Averaye Per Cent. of First Grade Enrollment Dropped out by End of Each Grade.*—Chicago.

GRADE.	AVERAGES OF 4 YEARS.		
	1880-83.	1884-87.	1888-91.
First	45.49	44.51	41.64
Second	54.58	57.76	50.99
Third	67.75	69.26	60.60
Fourth	76.04	76.84	....
Fifth	84.77	83.75	....
Sixth	90.08	89.65	....
Seventh	93.89	91.83	....
Eighth	96.36	....	....
Ninth	97.46	....	....
Tenth	98.49	....	....
Eleventh	99.06	....	....
Twelfth	100.00	....	....

TABLE XVIII.—*Influence of Death upon Duration of School Attendance.*

I. Grade.	II. Corresponding age.	III. Printed per cent. of deaths.	IV. Per cent. dropped out.	V. Per cent. remaining.	VI. Corrected per cent. of deaths.	VII. Total per cent. dropped by death.
First	7	92	43.29	100.00	.92	.92
Second	8	77	53.79	56.71	.43	1.35
Third	9	66	65.87	46.21	.30	1.65
Fourth	10	58	74.42	34.13	.20	1.85
Fifth	11	52	83.08	25.58	.13	1.98
Sixth	12	50	89.07	16.92	.08	2.06
Seventh	13	49	92.85	10.93	.05	2.11
Eighth	14	51	96.20	7.15	.04	2.15
Ninth	15	54	97.48	3.80	.020	2.170
Tenth	16	58	98.48	2.52	.013	2.183
Eleventh	17	64	99.06	1.52	.010	2.193
Twelfth	18	71	100.00	.94	.006	2.199

Table XIX.—*Enrollment by Classes.*—Milwaukee. Nineteen Years.

GRADE.	CLASS ENTERING IN THE SCHOOL YEAR—																		
	1878-79	1879-90	1880-81	1881-82	1882-83	1883-84	1884-85	1885-86	1886-87	1887-88	1888-89	1889-90	1890-91	1891-92	1892-93	1893-94	1894-95	1895-96	1896-97
First	4,435	5,004	4,550	3,296	5,588	6,135	5,823	5,777	6,240	6,098	6,843	7,114	7,474	7,639	7,915	7,570	7,078	7,418	7,359
Second	2,098	1,981	1,977	2,152	2,241	2,358	2,552	2,842	2,972	2,873	3,049	3,229	3,594	3,479	3,785	3,716	4,074	4,272	......
Third	2,041	1,961	1,876	2,008	2,295	2,280	2,319	2,398	2,549	2,536	2,667	2,833	3,042	3,306	3,348	3,541	3,744	......	......
Fourth	1,597	1,567	1,605	1,713	1,730	1,964	2,084	2,098	2,031	2,117	2,270	2,504	2,943	2,890	3,214	3,214	......	......	......
Fifth	1,199	1,100	1,168	1,290	1,308	1,520	1,685	1,687	1,592	1,695	1,792	2,130	2,426	2,574	2,846	......	......	......	......
Sixth	901	758	851	855	818	1,001	1,094	1,234	1,153	1,310	1,552	1,799	2,167	2,226	......	......	......	......	......
Seventh	594	518	534	557	536	683	734	855	866	1,111	1,348	1,477	1,737	......	......	......	......	......	......
Eighth	363	347	331	383	370	482	531	687	744	875	1,097	1,183	......	......	......	......	......	......	......

TABLE XX.—*Number Dropped Out by End of Each Grade.—Milwaukee.*

GRADE.	CLASS ENTERING IN THE SCHOOL YEAR—																		
	1878-79	1879-80	1880-81	1881-82	1882-83	1883-84	1884-85	1885-86	1886-87	1887-88	1888-89	1889-90	1890-91	1891-92	1892-93	1893-94	1894-95	1895-96	1896-97
First	2,337	3,023	2,573	3,141	3,344	3,777	3,271	2,935	3,268	3,225	3,794	3,885	3,880	4,160	4,130	3,854	3,001	3,146	......
Second	2,391	3,013	2,674	3,228	3,203	3,855	3,504	3,379	3,691	3,562	4,176	4,281	4,432	4,333	4,567	4,029	3,334	......	......
Third	2,833	3,437	2,945	3,583	3,858	4,171	3,789	3,679	4,200	3,981	4,573	4,610	4,531	4,749	4,701	4,356	......	......	......
Fourth	3,236	3,901	3,352	4,006	4,290	4,615	4,183	4,090	4,648	4,403	5,051	4,984	5,018	5,065	5,069	......	......	......	......
Fifth	3,534	4,246	3,699	4,441	4,770	5,134	4,729	4,543	5,082	4,788	5,291	5,315	5,307	5,413	......	......	......	......	......
Sixth	3,811	4,486	4,016	4,739	5,052	5,452	5,089	4,922	5,374	4,957	5,495	5,637	5,737	......	......	......	......	......	......
Seventh	4,072	4,657	4,219	4,913	5,218	5,653	5,292	5,090	5,496	5,223	5,746	5,931	......	......	......	......	......	......	......

TABLE XXI.—*Per Cent. of First Grade Enrollment Dropped out by End of Each Grade.*—Milwaukee.

GRADE.	CLASS ENTERING IN THE SCHOOL YEAR—																		Average.
	1878-79	1879-80	1880-81	1881-82	1882-83	1883-84	1884-85	1885-86	1886-87	1887-88	1888-89	1889-90	1890-91	1891-92	1892-93	1893-94	1894-95	1895-96	
First........	52.46	60.41	56.54	59.36	59.84	61.56	56.17	50.80	52.30	52.83	55.41	54.61	51.91	54.45	52.17	50.92	42.44	42.41	56.30
Second.....	53.98	60.31	58.87	60.93	53.92	62.83	60.17	58.49	59.21	58.39	61.02	60.17	59.29	56.72	57.70	53.22	47.10	......	59.49
Third.......	63.76	63.68	64.72	67.65	69.04	67.98	64.21	63.68	67.61	64.98	66.82	64.80	60.62	62.16	59.39	57.54	......	......	66.15
Fourth......	72.96	78.01	74.32	75.61	76.59	75.22	71.06	70.79	74.43	72.20	73.79	70.05	67.54	66.30	64.04	......	......	......	73.76
Fifth........	81.93	84.85	81.29	83.85	85.32	83.68	81.21	73.63	81.44	78.51	77.30	74.71	71.00	70.86	......	......	......	......	81.06
Sixth........	88.86	89.64	88.26	89.46	90.40	88.86	87.39	85.22	86.61	81.78	80.30	79.23	76.75	......	......	......	......	......	86.71
Seventh.....	91.83	93.06	92.72	92.76	93.37	92.14	90.89	88.10	88.07	85.64	83.96	83.51	......	......	......	......	......	......	89.93

Table XXII.— *Per Cent. that Dropped out after Corrections for Double Enrollment.* — Chicago.

(Illustrated for the middle year, 1886-87.)

GRADES.	ENROLLMENT FOR CLASS ENTER- ING IN 1886-87.			Per Cents as cor- rected.
	As Printed.	*As Corrected.*		
		By popula- tion.	Also by double en- rollment.	
First	27,954	27,954	15,374	30.89
Second	17,165	16,042	10,784	37.74
Third	14,579	12,766	9,574	44.23
Fourth	15,423	9,533	8,554	53.74
Fifth	13,191	7,111	7,111	65.87
Sixth	10,154	5,247	5,247	79.85
Seventh	6,310	3,127	3,127	82.35
Eighth	5,670	2,702	2,702	89.37
Ninth	3,598	1,635*	1,635	93.18
Tenth	2,408	1,047*	1,047	95.35
Eleventh	1,711	713*	713	....

* See Table X. Population in 1896 was 1,619,226.

TABLE XXIII.—*Final Conclusions as to Per Cents that Drop Out.*

GRADE.	By DEDUCTIVE METHOD.			By INDUCTIVE METHOD.		
	Chicago. " Mini-mum." (Table IX.)	Milwaukee. Not actual enrollment. (Table VII.)	Chicago. Actual enrollment. (Table IV.)	Chicago. Corrected for double enrollment. (Table XXII.)	Chicago. " Maxi-mum." (Table XVI.)	Milwaukee. Not actual enrollment. (Table XXI.)
First	27	35	32	31	43	56
Second	43	51	51	38	54	59
Third	58	65	66	44	66	66
Fourth	71	76	78	54	74	74
Fifth	82	85	86	66	83	81
Sixth........	89	91	92	80	89	87
Seventh	93	95	95	82	93	90
Eighth	96	97	97	89	96	....
Ninth	98.0	....	98.6	93.1	97.5	....
Tenth	99.0	....	99.3	95.4	98.5	....
Eleventh	99.6	....	99.7	....	99.1	....
Twelfth	100.0	....	100.0	100.0	100.0	....

TABLE XXIV.— *Public and Private Schools of Chicago, 1893-94.*

	TEACHERS.		PUPILS.			
	Male.	Female	Male.	Female	Under 21 yrs.	Over 21 yrs.
PUBLIC SCHOOLS.						
Primary and Grammar Departments....	124	3,427	....	....	178,884	....
High School.............................	99	102	....	....	6,189	....
Unclassified	32	28	....	....	285	....
Totals...............................	255	3,557	....	....	185,358	....
Evening Schools.........................	(410)		14,200	4,069	18,269	....
OTHER THAN PUBLIC SCHOOLS.						
Kindergarten............................	7	321	1,516	2,255	2,663	988
Private	99	201	2,335	2,594	4,520	459
Church or Parochial.....................	238	948	29,303	31,921	80,523	339
Other Educational Institutions	550	281	8,193	7,426	9,477	4,972
Totals...............................	894	1,751	41,397	44,196	77,183	6,758
Grand Totals (Public and Private Schools)	1,149	5,308	....	....	262,541	6,758

20

www.ingramcontent.com/pod-product-compliance
Lightning Source LLC
Chambersburg PA
CBHW031804090426
42739CB00008B/1154